BASIC DOCTRINES OF THE CHRISTIAN FAITH

WILLIAM N. BUSH

ECS MINISTRIES
The Word to the World

Many ECS publications are also available in eBook formats.
For more information, visit our website www.ecsministries.org.

Basic Doctrines of the Christian Faith

William N. Bush

Published by:
ECS Ministries
PO Box 1028
Dubuque, IA 52004-1028
phone: (563) 585-2070
email: ecsorders@ecsministries.org
website: www.ecsministries.org

First ECS Edition 2014
Reprinted 2015

ISBN 978-1-59387-221-2

Code: W-BDCF

Previously published by Walterick Publishers.

Printed in the United States of America

The Eternal God
The New Birth
The Church
Eternity

Contents

Author's Preface

IT IS HOPED that this booklet will be of value not only to teachers and personal workers, but also to new Christians, both young and old, as a help in exploring the Word of God and in becoming acquainted with the wonders and joys of belonging to Christ and being a part of His glorious bride and a member of "the church."

The author's prayer is that each one who uses it may find as much blessing in reading it and in the resulting meditation on God's precious Word as he found in putting it together.

–William N. Bush

A Statement of Faith

- In the Bible as the divinely inspired and inerrant Word of God, the revelation of God's mind and will to man, and that it is our infallible, all-sufficient guide for salvation and for the Christian life (2 Tim. 3:16-17, 2 Pet. 1:20-21).
- In one God, the Creator of all, eternally existing in three persons: Father, Son, and Holy Spirit.
- In the deity of the Lord Jesus Christ—that He is true God and true man begotten of the Holy Spirit, born of a virgin, and that He has a perfect and sinless humanity (John 1:1; Phil. 2:6; Matt. 1:23-25; 1 John 3:5).
- In the total depravity of the nature of man through his fall in the garden of Eden, and the absolute inability of man to save himself from eternal punishment by his own works (Genesis 3; Rom. 3:22-23; Eph. 2:8-9).
- In the bodily resurrection of the just and the unjust, the everlasting blessedness of the saved (1 Thess. 4:16-17); and the everlasting and conscious punishment of the lost (Rev. 20:11-15).
- In the sacrifice and finished work of Jesus Christ on the cross of Calvary (through which sacrifice Christ has effected complete and eternal redemption, God setting His seal of approval on Christ's work by raising Him out from among the dead and enthroning Him at His own right hand in heaven) and that Christ is the Head of the church, the Lord of the individual, the Great High Priest over the house of God, and Advocate in the family of God.

- In the immediate and eternal salvation of every person who truly believes on Christ and by faith rests on His finished work as the only righteous ground on which a Holy God can forgive his sins.
- That all who by faith receive the Lord Jesus Christ as Savior are born again of the Holy Spirit, indwelt by the Holy Spirit, and by the Holy Spirit baptized into the body of Christ, the church, of which Christ is the risen and ascended Head (1 Cor. 12:12-14; Eph. 1:22-23; Col. 1:18).
- That the early church met together and "continued steadfastly in the apostles' doctrine and fellowship, in the breaking of bread, and in prayers" (Acts 2:42), showing us God's pattern for the church today.
- In the personal, imminent, and pre-tribulational coming of the Lord to the air to rapture (catch up) the church (1 Thess. 4:13-17).
- In the revelation of Christ in glory at His second advent to the earth to establish His kingdom on earth and to reign in righteousness (2 Thess. 1:6-10; Phil. 2:9-11).

What does it mean that the Bible is "inspired"?

Understanding the meaning of *inspiration*, as well as believing without question in the truth and accuracy of every portion of the Bible, is absolutely essential for every born-again believer as a qualification for serving the Lord.

The word *inspiration* occurs only once in the New King James Version of the Bible:

2 Tim. 3:16-17: "All Scripture is given by *inspiration* of God, and is profitable for doctrine, for reproof, for correction, for instruction

in righteousness, that the man of God may be complete, thoroughly equipped for every good work."

Here the word means "God breathed." But repeatedly throughout the Scriptures are statements that the words recorded are the words of God Himself. Following are a few examples:

- "Then the LORD said to Moses . . ." (Ex. 6:1)
- "And the LORD said to Moses . . ." (Ex. 7:1)
- "And God spoke all these words, saying . . ." (Ex. 20:1)
- "The Spirit of the LORD spoke by me . . ." (2 Sam. 23:2)
- "But the LORD said to me . . ." (Jer. 1:7)
- ". . . which was spoken of the Lord by the prophet, saying, . . ." (Matt. 1:22)
- "For David himself said by the Holy Spirit . . ." (Mark 12:36)

Other Scriptures reinforce these evidences:

1 Peter 1:10-11: "Of this salvation the prophets have inquired and searched carefully, who prophesied of the grace that would come to you, searching what, or what manner of time, the Spirit of Christ who was in them was indicating when He testified beforehand the sufferings of Christ and the glories that would follow."

2 Peter 1:21: "For the prophecy never came by the will of man, but holy men of God spoke as they were moved by the Holy Spirit."

The dictionary defines inspiration theologically as "A supernatural divine influence on the prophets, apostles, or sacred writers by which they were qualified to communicate truth without error; a supernatural influence which qualified men to receive and communicate divine truth."

L. Gaussen, a 19th century Swiss Bible scholar, gave this definition:

> "That inexplicable power which the divine Spirit put forth of old on the authors of Holy Scripture, in order to their guidance even in the employment of the words they used, and to preserve them alike from all error and from all omission."

Inspiration is two-fold: *plenary*, as to the truths expressed; and *verbal*, as to the words used.

God used men to write the Bible—about forty, over a period about 1600 years. For example, He prepared

- Job, the patriarch
- Moses, the scholar and sheepherder
- Samuel, who heard the call of God
- David, the shepherd boy, warrior, and king
- Solomon, the wise man
- The prophets
- Luke, a physician
- John, who described himself as "the disciple whom Jesus loved"
- Paul, a doctor of the law
- Peter, a fisherman and devoted follower, who learned of the Lord's love and mercy by failure, experience, and companionship
- And others, as equally qualified by God.

God revealed His word and purposes and will to them, selected from their vocabularies the words He wanted used, totally inspired their writings—word and thought—but preserved the flavor of their personality in their revelation of His divine plan. Often they did not understand what they wrote, but they knew they were communicating His Word (1 Pet. 1:11-12).

Nothing is included in the Bible that He did not want there; nothing is missing that He wanted there. All Scripture—the entire Bible—is given by inspiration of God—it is God's Word to correct, to reprove, to instruct you (2 Tim. 3:16). We should not tamper with the contents of God's Word (Deut. 4:2; Prov. 30:6; Rev. 22:18-19).

Who comprises the Jews, the Gentiles, and the church of God? (1 Cor. 10:32)

Since creation, God has been dealing with man in both love and judgment. In the beginning, the relationship was one of love. He dealt with Adam and Eve in their innocence until they rebelled and sinned against Him. In their newly acquired "knowledge of good and evil," (Gen. 3:5) God dealt with them under conscience, but again man failed and God sent the flood (Genesis 6).

After the flood, God gave Noah and his descendents control of everything (Gen. 9:2-3) and based His relationship with them upon their newly acquired authority. But again they failed, at the Tower of Babel (Genesis 11). God confused their language and scattered them.

Next, God called a man called Abram to leave his country, his family, and his father's house, and travel to a land that He would show him (Gen. 12:1-2). He made a promise to Abram in Genesis 12:3, "I will bless those who bless you, and I will curse him who curses you; and in you all the families of the earth shall be blessed." Later God changed the name of Abram to Abraham. The later chapters of Genesis and the first chapters of Exodus record how Abraham's family grew in great numbers while living in Egypt and eventually left Egypt to return to the land God had promised them.

God then dealt with them in a new manner, giving them His law to guide and regulate every part of their lives and qualifying His promise (Exodus 20; Leviticus 26). His blessing and their enjoyment of His promises were dependent upon their obedience to His commandments. God re-emphasized this in Deuteronomy 31:14-30, warning them of severe judgment if they disobeyed. The history of the children of Israel—their successes and their failures and God's love and His judgment—fill the Old Testament and cannot be discussed in detail here. All can be summed up in a few words—they forsook God, were judged by God as warned, and carried captive into Babylon.

From the first captivity of the children of Israel about 600 BC to the birth of Christ, little is told us in the Bible except in Ezra, Nehemiah, Esther, and the prophets from Isaiah to Malachi. From Malachi (about 397 BC) to the birth of the Lord Jesus in 5 BC, nothing is told us in the Scriptures (Because of an error in calculation when our calendar was devised, Christ's birth, by that calendar, was in 5 BC. The date of December 25 is uncertain). During this period, the land of Israel and its people came under the control of the Roman Empire. Also, sometime during the six hundred years before the birth of the Lord Jesus, the ten tribes that were the nation of Israel lost their identity; they are often referred to as "the lost ten tribes." But God knows where they are and He will bring them back to the land in His good time. Only two tribes, Judah and Benjamin, retained their identity. The term *Jews* as applied to God's chosen people is a contraction of the name *Judah* and was first applied to those in the nation of Judah (Judah and Benjamin) with their capital at Jerusalem. The ten tribes were called

"Israel," and their capital was called Samaria. As a name, *Jews* is first found in the Bible in 2 Kings 16:6. Later, and in New Testament times, the term included all the children of Israel.

The Jews failed totally when they rejected the Lord Jesus, their Messiah (Anointed One), at the cross. During the period from the call of Abraham to the cross, Abraham and his descendants were God's "chosen" people, the special object of His love and care. All other people groups were (and are) *Gentiles*. In the New Testament, Gentiles are sometimes referred to as "Greeks" because of the universal use of the Greek language, as contrasted with Hebrew. See Romans 1:14, 16, and 10:12.

God set the Jews aside because of their rejection of Christ (see Lev. 26:14-39). He began to deal with man in a totally new and different way, in grace. This is explained very clearly by the apostle Paul in Ephesians 2:11-22. As stated in John 3:16, the love of God now flows out equally to all mankind, both Jews and Gentiles. All can come to God the same way: through faith in the Lord Jesus Christ and His atoning death on the cross. Christ is the way to God for all (John 14:6). Those who come through simple faith in the finished work of Christ become members of the *church of God*.

But there is one final comment: God has not forsaken Israel—the Jews—forever, and nor has He forgotten His promise to Abraham. There are two parts to His promise; one part has been fulfilled, and the other is yet to be fulfilled:

1. God has fulfilled Genesis 22:18: "In your seed all the nations of the earth will be blessed." Paul describes the fulfillment this way, in Galatians 3:8-9, "And the Scripture, foreseeing that God would justify the Gentiles by faith, preached the gospel to Abraham beforehand, saying, 'In you all the nations shall

be blessed.' So then, *those who are of faith are blessed* with believing Abraham" (italics added). See also Isaiah 53; John 3:16; and Hebrews 9:26-28; 10:1-14.

2. God will again resume His relationship with Israel, His chosen people, restoring them after they repent of their national sin of rejecting Jesus Christ. There is much in the Bible about this, but only one reference will be given here—Rom. 11:1-36, especially verse 26.

What is man's relationship to God by natural birth?

Man, as born into the world, is a sinner, a rebel against God, in both his nature and his actions. He is unfit for God's presence and cannot enter heaven in his natural condition; nor can he, by his own works or efforts, make himself fit for heaven (Rom. 3:23; 5:12; 7:18; 8:8; Eph. 2:1-3; 2:8-9; Rev. 21:27).

How can man become acceptable to God?

Man can do nothing to become acceptable to God; it is God who has provided a way for man to be acceptable to Him, to give him a righteous standing in His presence. Redemption, forgiveness of sins, cleansing from all unrighteousness and guilt, and eternal life are provided for those who put their trust in the Lord Jesus to save them. This is possible through the mystery of the *incarnation*—that is, the Son of God became man through the virgin birth while never ceasing to be God. He *could not* sin, because there was no sin in His nature. He lived a sinless life—one free from sin in word, deed or thought—unspotted by the sin around Him. On the cross God judged Him for the sin of every man, woman, and child. He voluntarily sacrificed Himself as our substitute and was judged in our place, paying the just penalty due for our sin by His death. In Galatians 2:20, Paul writes, "the Son of God loved me and gave Himself for me." See also John 3:16 and Hebrews 9:12-15; 10:4, 12-18.

What is the new birth?

The person who puts his trust in the Lord Jesus Christ as Savior is "born again," receiving eternal life as a gift from God. Just as a man receives natural life through natural birth, so he receives spiritual, eternal life when he believes in Christ and in His atoning death. The receiving of this new life is called *the new birth*. It is not imparted by any power in man but by the power of God (John 1:12-13). In the same way a man lives a natural life because of his natural birth and nothing he does has any effect on, or contributes anything to, that natural birth, so a man has and lives the new life by the power of God and nothing he does contributes anything to the new birth itself or generates it. He lives the new life because he has been born again. Birth always comes before life; one cannot live until he is born. Refer to John 1:10-13; 3:3-8; Galatians 2:20; and 1 Peter 1:23.

How can a person be sure he is born again and that his sins are forgiven?

This is a matter of believing what God says in His written Word. To believe is to be sure—fully persuaded—without doubt or reservation, that God means everything He says in the Bible and that He will do everything He says. Assurance is based not on *feeling* saved, but on trusting God's promises. Salvation (forgiveness, the new life, being born again) is certain because it rests on the finished work of the Lord Jesus Christ at Calvary (John 19:30) and upon the promise of God—God who never changes and never lies (Titus 1:2). "He that has the Son *has* life" (1 John 5:12). It is the positive and present possession of one who believes (1 John 5:13; Matt. 11:28; John 3:36; 5:24; 6:37; Rom. 8:1; 1 Pet. 1:2-5).

A warning is in order here, however. Although the Holy Spirit (a person of the Godhead) comes to dwell permanently in the believer the moment he or she believes (see John 14:16, 17, 26; 16:13-16; Rom. 8:23; 1 Cor. 6:19-20; 2 Cor. 1:22; 5:5; Eph. 1:13-14), God does not remove "our old man," our sinful nature; instead He provides a way for us to cope with it, to be delivered from its dominion (Rom. 6:1-23; Gal. 2:20). Deliverance from the control by the old nature is a constant battle, as evident from the apostle Paul's comments in Romans 7:14-25.

It is possible to have the victory now, but the final, total victory comes when we are caught up to be forever with the Lord (1 Thess. 4:13-18) and are changed into His likeness (Phil. 3:20-21; 1 John 3:2). At that point we shall be delivered from the old nature and the "body of sin" (Rom. 6:6; cf. 1 Cor. 15:51-58).

We have been warned that the natural desire to sin has not been eradicated from our nature (Rom. 7:18; 8:8). We should not allow sin to control our actions, but if we do sin, there is a provision for the forgiveness of sins committed by us after we have trusted Christ as Savior (1 John 1:8-10). We should confess our sins as soon as we are aware that we have committed them. For full enjoyment of our fellowship with the Father and His Son, we must "keep short accounts" with God—never let known sin go unconfessed. See Psalm 24:3-5; 66:18. We are counseled to judge ourselves to avoid being judged (1 Cor. 11:31-32). At God's right hand we have One to plead our cause, One to whom we belong, our Advocate, Jesus Christ the Righteous (1 John 2:1).

Who is the Holy Spirit?

The Holy Spirit (Luke 11:13; 35), also called the Spirit (John 1:33), the Spirit of Truth (John 14:17), the Comforter (John 14:26), the Spirit of God (1 Cor. 3:16), is One of the three persons of the Trinity, or Godhead

(Acts 17:29). He is not an influence but a *person,* divine, infinite and eternal, just as are God the Father, and God the Son.

During Old Testament times, the Spirit came upon men and women to direct their activities for God (Judges 13:25; 15:14; 16:20). In reply to Mary's question in Luke 1:34 as to how she, a virgin, could have a child, the angel Gabriel replied: "The Holy Spirit will come upon you, and the power of the Highest will overshadow you; therefore, also, that Holy One who is to be born will be called the Son of God" (Luke 1:35).

The Lord Jesus was subject to the Holy Spirit throughout His incarnation (John 1:33, Luke 4:1, 14, 18). This was true even when He died on the cross (Heb. 9:14).

The Holy Spirit is in the world now to reprove (convict) the world of sin, of righteousness, and of judgment (John 16:8-11). He is given to and dwells in all who are born again as a pledge, or guarantee, of their possession of eternal life. The Bible says those who believe are "sealed with that Holy Spirit of promise, who is the guarantee of our inheritance . . ." (Eph. 1:13-14).

The Lord Jesus promised His disciples the gift of the Holy Spirit, One who would live in them forever, to guide them into all truth, to teach them all things, to bring the Lord's words to their remembrance, and reveal to them things to come (John 14:16-17, 26; 15:26; 16:13-14). We can claim these promises today if we are believers in Christ. The Holy Spirit came to dwell in all the believers on the day of Pentecost after the Lord's ascension (Acts 2, compare John 7:39). The believer's body is the temple of the Holy Spirit—it is the believer's responsibility to glorify God in his body (1 Cor. 6:19-20). A believer can resist, grieve, quench, and even lie to the Holy Spirit (Acts 7:51; Eph. 4:30; 1 Thess. 5:19; Acts 5:3), but the Holy Spirit will never leave him (John 14:16). There is an interesting passage in 2 Thessalonians 2:7-12 concerning "He who now restrains" the devil and the power of evil, that "He will do so until he is taken out of the way." Many Bible students believe the restraining power is the church and the indwelling Holy Spirit in each believer. When the church is caught up by the Lord (1 Thess. 4:13-18), the restraining power will be removed and the awful times of the great tribulation will come (see—*What and when will the great tribulation take place?* below).

What is eternal security?

The words are simple: *eternal,* meaning "forever, without end, and *security,* meaning "beyond the reach of danger; safety, freedom from doubt, no fear, certainty."

The Lord Jesus promised eternal safety, or security, to those who put their trust in Him to save them from their sins (John 5:24; 6:37; 10:27-30; 14:19; Rom. 8:1).

Works have no part in securing our salvation—it is the gift of God to those who, conscious of their sin (their nature) and their sins (their acts) which bar them from heaven (Rev. 21:27), trust the Lord Jesus as Savior without any doubt or reservation (John 5:24; 3:14-18, 36; Rom. 6:23; Eph. 2:8-9).

We have the assurance of eternal security because God promises it (1 John 5:13). In this verse, it is stated that one *knows* he has (present possession) eternal life as a free gift on the basis of believing on the name of the Son of God—nothing else is added to "believing." It is God's promise—and God never changes (Mal. 3:6) or lies (Heb. 6:18).

To believe is to be sure in one's heart, without doubt or reservation, that God means and will do everything that He says (Heb. 6:17-20). See also John 5:24; 10:27-30. God has said in John 3:16, ". . . should not perish, but *have* everlasting life" (italics added). That statement is enough, giving total assurance (John 1:10-13; 1 Pet. 1:23).

What is the church, and how does a person become a member?

The original meaning of the word translated "church" in the Bible is a word used by the Greeks for a body of citizens gathered to discuss the affairs of state (see Acts 19:39).

In the Bible, it means either

(a) The entire company of believers throughout the era from Pentecost to the coming of Christ for all the redeemed, both living and dead. Christ was referring to this company when He said, ". . . I will build My church . . ." (Matt. 16:18); or

(b) A company of believers in a given location (see Acts 20:17; 1 Cor. 1:2; Gal. 1:2; 1 Thess. 1:1; etc). All believers, including those in a local church, are members of the *church universal*, which includes all born-again believers regardless of any earthly association they may have.

One may be associated with some local group or assembly of professing Christians or with some large religious organization, either national or worldwide, but such association, in itself, will not make one a member of *the church,* which is described in Scripture as

- The body of Christ (Eph. 1:22-23; Col. 1:24)
- The bride of Christ (Rev. 21:9)
- The building, a "holy temple in the Lord" (Eph. 2:14-22)

The church is composed of all born-again believers. God alone places the members in the church. He places them in the body in the place where He wants them to be (Acts 2:47; 1 Cor. 12:18-20).

What is the "body," the "bride," and the "building"?

The church is referred to Christ's *body* in relationship to Him as the Head of the church (Eph. 1:18-23; 4:1-6, 12; 5:23-32; Col. 2:18-19; Rom. 12:4; 1 Cor. 12:7-27).

The church is referred to as the *bride* of Christ in her nearness to Him, and her eternal relationship to Him (Eph. 5: 22-32; Rev. 19:7-8; 21:9).

The church is referred to as a *building*, built by the Lord Jesus of living stones to be a spiritual house for the purpose of offering up "spiritual sacrifices" (1 Cor. 3:9-17; Eph. 2:19-22; 1 Pet. 2:4-6). The church is built upon Christ as its foundation (1 Cor. 3:10-23) and He is the chief cornerstone (1 Pet. 2:4-7).

Why is each assembly, or local church, autonomous (not responsible to an earthly head or board)?

According to Scripture, Christ is the Head of the church (Eph. 1:22-23). He is also the Mediator between God and men (1 Tim. 2:5-6). No mere man has any right to interpose himself between God and men or to stand between the Lord Jesus and men. As one studies the writings of the apostles Paul, Peter, and John in the Bible, one finds no human head (singular) in control of any local church or assembly. Nor does one find a general human head over the church universal. The elders or bishops (always spoken of in the plural) provide *leadership* in the local church. These men are motivated by the Spirit of God and by love for the members of the body of Christ; they are specially gifted of God for this leadership and, having this gift, are recognized by those in the church. In the days of the early church, the relationship the apostles and others who ministered the Word of God had with the various local churches or assemblies was individual with each church; it was not conducted through any supervising head. There were some who aspired to grasp control, like Diotrephes, "who loves to have the preeminence among them" and refused to receive the apostle John (3 John 9-10). He was condemned by John as out of order.

In Colossians 2:18-19 Paul wrote, Let no one cheat you of your reward, taking delight in false humility and worship of angels, intruding into those things which he has not seen, vainly puffed up by his fleshly mind, and not holding fast to the Head, from whom all the body, nourished and knit together by joints and ligaments, grows with the increase that is from God." In Colossians 2:10 he wrote, "And you are complete in Him, who is the head of all principality and power," and in Colossians 3:11 he wrote ". . . Christ is all, and in all."

First Timothy chapter 3; 1 Thessalonians 5:12-13; Titus 1:5; and 1 Peter 5:1-4 indicate that each local church had local government under the leadership of bishops or elders who were given the gifts to lead, shepherd and teach by God Himself, and who were responsible to God, not to any earthly head (Acts 15:4-6, Eph. 4:1-16, 1 Tim. 5:17).

Why do the assemblies use no denominational name?

According to Ephesians 4:4 there is "one body"—see also 1 Corinthians 12:12-27. Paul especially condemns separation of the church into various divisions. He asks, "Is Christ divided?" (1 Cor. 1:1-13; 3:1-23). The only name for the church of God—the church in which God places *all* who believe (Acts 2:47) must be a name of God's choosing, a name which includes *all* the redeemed, a name which does not separate or divide. Obviously, this cannot be the name of a man or the name of a distinguishing belief or practice or doctrine, but a name to which *all* born-again believers can subscribe. The names we find in God's Word which qualify are

- Christians (Acts 11:26)
- Believers (Acts 5:14)
- Brethren (Acts 15:22; 22:5; Rom. 16:14)
- Saints (Acts 9:32; Rom. 16:15)

Read Mark 3:25; Romans 16:17-18; and 1 Corinthians 1:9-13; 3:1-23; 11:18, which all speak to the importance of warnings against division.

Why should there be no specially designated pastor or head of a local assembly?

The unique position the Head of the church is filled only by the Lord Jesus (Eph. 1:20-23; 4:4-6; Matt. 23:8-10). God's form of government is not a democracy, and neither is it a monarchy. It is a theocracy, ruled *by* God *for* God.

God rules His church on earth through His representatives—that is, born-again believers who do the work of elders or bishops in the local church. See Acts 14:23; 15:4-6, 23; 16:4; 20:17; Philippians 1:1; 1 Timothy 3:1; 5:17; Titus 1:5; and 1 Peter 5:1-3.

The term *pastor* as referring to a man (a shepherd or feeder) is so translated only once in the New Testament—in Ephesians 4:11. It does not refer to the head of a church, but to one who shepherds or feeds the believers. The sixteen other times this word appears in the New Testament it is translated "shepherd." Nine times it is used of a natural or human shepherd who takes care of literal sheep, and seven times it refers to the Lord Jesus as the Shepherd. Those mentioned in Ephesians 4:11 who minister in various ways to the believers (apostles, prophets, evangelists, pastors, teachers) are given (gifted and appointed) by the Lord to serve the church, but in all things He, the Lord, has the preeminence (Col. 1:18). No man is a ruler or lord—the way he leads is *by example* (1 Pet. 5:1-3).

The instruction to the church at Thessalonica is for us today as well: to "recognize those who labor among you, and are over you in the Lord, and admonish you; and to esteem them very highly in love for their work's sake" (1 Thess. 5:12-13). We are told to follow and obey them (Heb. 13:7, 17). Again it must be emphasized that pastors are among those given to the church by God "for the equipping of the saints for the work of ministry, for the edifying of the body of Christ" (Eph. 4:12). These pastors are a gift to the entire church to teach and guide the believers, but the Lord Jesus is "the head over all things to the church" (Eph. 1:22).

Who are elders (bishops) and deacons? What is their work?

There are two groups of believers who are responsible for leading and conducting the affairs of the local church or assembly—elders (also called bishops) and deacons. The word *elder* indicates maturity. These men of mature spiritual experience serve as overseers, or superintendents, of the assembly in all spiritual affairs. They are not elected, chosen, or appointed by men, but motivated by the Spirit of God to serve as spiritual guides of the local church. They do this by leading (by example), shepherding, teaching, and watching for the spiritual welfare of the believers—not for money, but out of love for God and the believers. They are always referred to in the plural—more than one. They are to do their work willingly, not by constraint (1 Pet. 5:1-3; 1 Thess. 5:12-13; Heb. 13:17). Elders are to be honored and esteemed for "their work's sake" (1 Thess. 5:13; 1 Tim. 5:1, 19), not for their personality or human attainments. Their qualifications are given in 1 Timothy 3:1-7 and Titus 1:6-9.

These men (elders or bishops) work in harmony and unity with each other, seeking the guidance of God through prayer and searching of God's Word. The gifts God gives each one complement the gifts He gives the others. Godly elders, by their counsel and guidance, keep the assembly in fellowship with the Lord and with one another. Again it must be emphasized that these men are known for their labor among God's people and the believers are exhorted to remember them, follow them, and obey them (Heb. 13:7, 17, 24).

The word *deacon* means "minister" or "servant." They are to serve in the church. Deacons administered the physical or temporal affairs of the local church. Following the example set in Acts 6:1-8, deacons are to be appointed. You will note from the account in Acts 6 that the first deacons were chosen because they were "men of good reputation, full of the Holy Spirit and wisdom"—not just men who had been successful in business. It is significant to notice that one of those selected (Stephen) was "full of faith and power," and "did great wonders and miracles among the people." Another, Philip, was a most effective evangelist (Acts 8:5-40). But God's regard for them is evident in their qualifications given in 1 Timothy 3:8-13. These qualifications are very similar to those of the elders, the two noticeable omissions in those of the deacons being "hospitable [and] able to teach" (1 Tim. 3:2). Of the deacons it is said, "For those who have served well as deacons obtain for themselves a good standing and great boldness in the faith which is in Christ Jesus" (1 Tim. 3:13).

It must be pointed out again that both elders and deacons were always referenced in the plural.

Why do we not take an offering at church meetings where non-Christians may be present?

There is a natural human belief that "giving to God" will cause God to be favorably disposed to the giver, but that is a false assumption (Titus 3:5). Salvation—forgiveness of sins—is a free gift from God (Rom. 6:23; Eph. 2:8-9). Since God has offered salvation as a gift, it is not consistent for us to place a "price tag" on that gift. The Lord Jesus said, ". . . freely you have received, freely give" (Matt. 10:8). In no way should a local congregation of believers suggest the thought that giving anything to God has any part in salvation or the forgiveness of sins. We do not want to give anyone the thought that by giving they can merit God's salvation—read Acts 8:18-24. The gospel and the ministry of God's Word should therefore be free and without cost to those who are not saved. In this instance, if Peter had accepted the money, it would have given Simon a false hope.

One must belong to God before one can give to God (2 Cor. 8:1-5). God does not need our gifts but He receives them from those who belong to Him (Ps. 50:9-17; Rom. 12:1-2).

When *do* we take an offering? At the worship service—the Lord's Supper. Why? Because usually only believers are at this meeting of the church (Acts 2:41-44; 5:13-14; 1 Cor. 16:1-2). God's work is carried on without support (financial help) from unsaved persons (3 John 7; 2 Cor. 6:14).

Who is the Center of our gathering?

This can be answered in one word—*Christ.* He is the Head over all things to the church (Eph. 1:22-23). We do not gather to a program, nor to a man of pleasing personality, nor to a building, nor to an organization or an association, but to the living, exalted, person of the Lord Jesus Christ (Matt. 18:20; John 15:4-6; Eph. 1:9-12, 22-23;

4:4-16; Col. 1:12-23; Heb. 13:13—see also Phil. 2:9-11). There also are two other verses that are very interesting concerning the preeminent Son of God as the gathering center—John 11:51-52 and Genesis 49:10.

Who should be baptized? When should it be done, how, and why?

Baptism in water is a picture (symbol) of our salvation from sin; of death to the power and control of sin and of living now in Christ's resurrection power. Every Christian should be baptized because Christ commanded His followers to be baptized (Matt. 28:19-20). It is associated with conversion to Christ and follows it. Just as nothing we "do" contributes to our physical birth, but follows it, so baptism is not a part of being born again or converted, but follows it.

As believers in Christ, we are to reckon that the "old man" (Rom. 6:6) died with Christ (Gal. 2:20). What do we do with dead things? We bury them. Baptism pictures our burial with Christ when He died and received in His body God's condemnation of sin. In being baptized we are identifying with Christ in His death. We come up from the waters of baptism, having already received salvation through faith in Christ, to walk in newness of life with Christ. We are to consider ourselves as dead to self, sin, and the world, and alive to the Lord (Rom. 6:3-11). It is a testimony—a raising of the flag—to tell the world that we are new creatures in Christ Jesus. The actual meaning of the Greek word from which *baptize* comes is "to immerse, or plunge." A body is not buried until it is dead, and when it *is* buried it is entirely covered—a few handfuls of earth do not constitute burial. Thus we believe in baptism by immersion (Act 8:36-39). Baptism is obedience by the believer and a testimony to the world (Matt. 28:19-20; Acts 9:18, 10:47, Rom. 6:1-13, Gal. 2:20).

Why do we observe the Lord's Supper? When and how often should we do it?

The Lord's Supper, often called "The Breaking of Bread" or "The Remembrance Meeting," is celebrated or participated in at the special request of the Lord Jesus. We do it in memory of Him and His giving Himself as our substitute on the cross to be the sacrifice for our atonement. He offered Himself both as a sin offering and as a burnt offering to God (a study of the Levitical offerings will explain the significance of these).

The act of remembrance is to be done as He instituted it. It involves giving of thanks for and partaking of bread, which is a picture (symbol) of His body given for us on the cross and giving of thanks for and partaking of "the cup," a picture of His blood shed for us, the new testament (covenant, agreement) in His blood (Luke 22:20). Both the bread and the cup are for born-again believers (1 Cor. 11:27-29). The Lord Jesus said, "Do this in remembrance of Me" (Luke 22:19). We cannot remember someone we do not know, so this is only for those who "know" Him (that is, genuine believers).

The apostle Paul wrote in 1 Corinthians 11:26, "For as often as you eat this bread and drink this cup, you proclaim the Lord's death until He comes." It is evident from the book of Acts that the early church observed the Lord's Supper on the first day of the week (Acts 20:7). Possibly it may have been done more often. It was intimately associated with the regular activities of the church, and was so important that apparently the apostle Paul remained at Troas for seven days so that he could "break bread" with them (Acts 20:6-7) although he wanted to reach Jerusalem as soon as possible (Acts 20:15-17). The importance of the Lord's Supper is further emphasized by the special revelation given to Paul regarding it as mentioned in 1 Corinthians 11:23-34. For other references, see Matthew 26:26-28; Mark 14:22-24; Luke 22:15-20; and Acts 2:41-42; 20:7.

What is "fellowship"?

The dictionary gives the definition of *fellowship* as "A group of people with the same interests; a mutual sharing, as of experience, activity, interest; companionship; friendly association." The word as used in the New Testament means communion, or sharing in common. It is an intimate spiritual relationship between the Lord Jesus and the Christian, making it possible for us to enjoy His companionship and love. This relationship also extends to association among the people of God (1 John 1:3; 7; 3:14). Acts 2:44-47 illustrates fellowship: "All who believed were together, and had all things in common." They were of "one accord." There was no discord, no rivalry, no envy, no conflict (James 4:1), but rather total unity—see Psalm 133. The basis of fellowship is the redeeming work of the Lord Jesus Christ at Calvary and the indwelling Holy Spirit within each Christian (1 Cor. 6:19-20). This unites us in a common bond to the Lord Jesus and to one another, as we are all part of the body of Christ.

What is meant by the term "the priesthood of all believers"?

The Lord Jesus is our Great High Priest and our Advocate at God's right hand (Heb. 4:14, 1 John 2:1). See Hebrews 4:14-16, 7:19-28, 9-11-28, and 10:11-22.

We read in Revelation 5:10 that Christ "has made us kings and priests to our God." See also Revelation 1:6. Only our Great High Priest is between us and God (1 Tim. 2:5-6). Read again Hebrews 10:19-22. Each born-again believer has the same privilege to come near to God through our Great High Priest, the Lord Jesus Christ. No man has any right to seek to stand between the believer and the Lord Jesus. As a confirmation, read Revelation 20:6.

Simply stated, the priesthood of all believers means that every born-again believer is designated a priest and has the privilege and the responsibility to function as such. The moment an individual trusts the Lord Jesus as his Savior, is made a holy priest (1 Peter 2:5) to "worship the Lord in the beauty of holiness" (Ps. 29:2) and a royal priest (1 Peter 2:9) to perform practical service for the Lord Jesus (1 Peter 2:1-10).

Which is the most important meeting, or service, of the assembly?

As we examine the Scriptures we find that ministry to God (worship) commands the highest priority in all our service and in our relationship to God. Ministry to the people of God (manward)—service to the church—does not reach the high pinnacle of worship of God and of His beloved Son. The Lord's Supper—remembering Him—was a personal request made by the Lord Jesus Himself to His own. It is a meeting *with* Him, being occupied with Him alone, that prepares and sanctifies us for all other service.

> "In Ezekiel 44, God permitted the Levites that had gone into idolatry to minister "to the house" (the temple) but in Ezekiel 44:15-16, it was only the priests who had remained faithful when the children of Israel went astray who were permitted to minister to God. In Ezekiel 8:11-18, we find there can be activity in God's house and yet that activity can be filled with idolatry. It must be God first."
>
> –J. Boyd Nicholson

In 1 Peter 2:1-10, believers we are spoken of as holy priests (to offer up spiritual sacrifices, acceptable to God by Jesus Christ) before we are royal priests (to show forth the praises of Him who hath called us out of darkness into His marvelous light).

In Acts 2:41-44 "they [the believers] continued steadfastly in the apostles' doctrine and fellowship, and in breaking of bread, and in prayers." None of these was considered second-rate, none was slighted or left undone. Each is a part of our service for Him, it is all one package (Heb. 10:19-25). But worship is the highest privilege of all.

Who is the Trinity?

Although the word *Trinity* does not occur in the Bible, the Trinity—God, the Father; God, the Son; and God, the Holy Spirit is revealed in the pages of Holy Scripture from Genesis to Revelation—God, Three in One. The first verse in the Bible, Genesis 1:1 ("In the beginning God created the heavens and the earth") presents God as more than two persons. In the Hebrew language, nouns can exist in three forms—singular (one), dual (two), and plural (more than two). The word used for God in Genesis 1:1 is the plural form (more than two). Again we have this same word for God (*Elohim*—more than two) coupled with "LORD," or Jehovah, in Genesis 3:8-9, 13-14. This is the Trinity. It was the Triune God who created in Genesis 1:1. In Genesis 1:26, this same Triune God (*Elohim*) said, "Let *us* make man in *our* image . . ." (italics added).

In Luke 1:35 the angel Gabriel said to Mary, "The Holy Spirit will come upon you, and the power of the Highest will overshadow you: therefore, also, that Holy One who is to be born will be called the Son of God." In Matthew 28:19 we read, "Baptizing them in the name of the Father and of the Son and of the Holy Spirit." In Hebrews 9:14 it is recorded: ". . . Christ, who through the eternal Spirit offered Himself without spot to God . . ." Each member of the Trinity participated in the resurrection of the Lord Jesus—God the Father (Acts 13:29-30); the Holy Spirit (Rom. 8:11); and the Son (John 2:19-21; 10:17-18). In John 10:30 the Lord Jesus said, "I and My Father are one" and in John 1:32 we read that at His baptism, the Holy Spirit "remained upon Him."

These and many other Scriptures assert the truth of the triune God, and there are many evidences that Jesus is God and the Spirit is God.

Who is the devil?

The devil (Satan) is the enemy of God and man; he is the one who brought sin into the world (Gen 3:1-24). He was the one who tried to wreck Job's life and testimony (Job chapters 1 and 2). He was the one who moved Herod to kill the children in Bethlehem in an effort to destroy the Lord Jesus (Matt. 2:7-23). He was one who failed in his attempt in the wilderness to derail the Lord Jesus from His mission on earth (Luke 4:1-13). He was the one who entered into Judas and moved him to betray Jesus to the Jewish authorities (Luke 22:3).

What was his origin? Ezekiel 28:12-19 and Isaiah 14:12-15 seem to explain it. He was created as the anointed cherub—full of wisdom and beauty—perfect in his ways from the day he was created—until iniquity was found in him (Ezek. 28:15). His heart was lifted up because of his beauty. He said, "I will exalt my throne above the stars of God," "I will be like the Most High." He was cast out of heaven because of his rebellion. In Scripture He is referred to as

- A murderer and father of lies (John 8:44)
- That old serpent, the devil, Satan (Rev. 12:9)
- The god of this world (2 Cor. 4:4)
- Treacherous and deceitful; appearing as an angel of light (Rev. 12:9; 2 Cor. 11:14)
- Like a roaring lion, seeking to wreck the Christian's life and testimony (1 Pet. 5:8)
- Destructive, like a wolf preying on sheep (John 10:12)

God bruised Satan's head at Calvary (Gen. 3:15), yet Satan is still at large; he is active as the god of this world (2 Cor. 4:4). He is the one who will take over after the rapture of the church (2 Thess. 2:1-12). He is the great dragon, the dragon who gives power to the first beast (Rev. 13:1-10; the two beasts and the dragon are the diabolic counterfeit of the Trinity). He is the one who will gather the kings of the earth and their armies to the battle of Armageddon (Rev. 16:16; 19:11-21). He will be bound and cast into the bottomless pit for 1,000 years during the millennium (Rev. 20:1-3). When he is released after the millennium he will deceive the nations and gather them together to battle against the saints and the beloved city. Fire will come down from God out of heaven and devour them. The devil will be cast into the lake of fire forever, "where the beast and the false prophet are" (Rev. 20:7-10). Be warned that Satan does not always act depraved or immoral—he knows the language of heaven and he is alive and active today in many church pulpits (2 Cor. 11:13-15).

> "He [Satan] is not a cartoon character to be joked about. He is still the mightiest created being—that rank has not yet been stripped from him—see Dan. 10:12-13."
>
> –J. Boyd Nicholson

What and when is "the rapture"?

The dictionary gives the meaning of the word *rapture* as "the state of being carried away with joy, love, etc." with a rare meaning of "being carried away in body or spirit." While the word itself is not found in the Bible, it is used to designate the coming of the Lord Jesus to the air to "catch away" the church, His bride as foretold or alluded to in 1 Thessalonians 4:13-18; 1 Corinthians 15:51-58; John 14:1-3; Philippians 3:20-21; and 1 John 3:1-2. The Lord Jesus is coming to remove the church from the earth before the great tribulation that they might be eternally with Him in glory (John 17:24; 1 Thess. 4:17; 2 Thess. 2:1-12; Rev. 21:27–Rev. 22:5).

The rapture is the next event in prophecy to be fulfilled. It will mark the termination of the day of grace and will start again the chain of prophecy. It could occur at any moment and *will* occur before the great tribulation. There are some who believe the rapture will occur after the tribulation, thus subjecting the church to great suffering, and some who believe in a "partial rapture" (some of the church being caught away before the tribulation and some being left to go through that awful suffering).

These teachings are contrary to Scripture. Consider the following references: John 14:1-3; 17:24; Acts 1:11; 1 Corinthians 15:12-28, 51-55; 2 Corinthians 5:1-4; 2 Thessalonians 2:1-12; James 5:7-8; and 1 John 2:28; 3:2. Revelation 4:1 (in fact, all of Revelation chapters 4 and 5) indicates that the church is in heaven before the tribulation, and Revelation 19:6-21 clearly shows the bride (the church) to be in heaven with the Lord and accompanying Him as He comes forth to do battle and conquer His enemies, closing out the period of the great tribulation. First Thessalonians 3:13 implies that the church is with the Lord Jesus Christ at His coming with all His saints, thus indicating that the church will be taken to be with Him before the tribulation.

When the Lord comes at the rapture, all members of the church who have died will be raised and, together with all living members of the church, will be caught up (1 Thess. 4:13-18) and changed into His likeness (1 Cor. 15:51-55; 1 John 3:2)—bodies changed and glorified, within and without (the conformity more than physical), to be like Him.

What and when is the great tribulation?

The *great tribulation* comes during the seven-year period immediately after the rapture. This seven-year period is Daniel's "seventieth week" (Dan. 9:24-27). The awful outpouring of God's judgment on those who have rejected the Lord Jesus and are alive at the time will occur during the last three and half years of this seven-year period (Dan. 9:27). This is called the "time of Jacob's trouble" in Jeremiah 30:1-24.

The nation of Israel will be punished for rejecting the Lord Jesus as the One God chose to be their Ruler (Dan. 12:1-3; Zech. 13:1-9; Rev. 1:7; Revelation chapters 6–18). The unbelieving among the Gentile nations also will be punished. Many (more than half the population of the world) will die under the wrath of God. But men will continue to rebel against God, blaspheming God and remaining unrepentant (Rev. 6:6-17; 16:10-11, 21).

However, many of Israel will repent (Revelation 7), as well as many Gentiles of every nation (Rev. 5:9; 7:9; Dan 12:1-3; Ezek. 34). The "everlasting gospel" will be preached and many will turn to God and be saved from eternal damnation (Rev. 14:6-13; 6:9-11; 20:4-6). Although these will not be part of the church, they will live and be blessed eternally.

The great tribulation will end with the coming of the Lord, visible to all as King of kings and Lord of lords, to judge the living nations at the great battle of Armageddon. The Lord will have a glorious victory; the "beast and the false prophet" will be cast alive into the lake of fire; the devil will be bound and cast into the bottomless pit for a thousand years; and the millennial reign of Christ will begin (Rev. 19:11 to Rev. 20:6).

Is there only one final judgment?

Many people in the world who have any belief in God or in existence after death have a confused and uncertain impression that there will be one final judgment of all, at which time everyone's deeds will be judged—the good works weighed against the bad—to determine what one's eternal fate will be. Nothing could be further from the truth. There is no basis in the Bible for such a belief. Much could be said about this, but comments here will be confined to the following brief discussion.

There is a very startling statement in John 3:18—"He who believes in Him [the Lord Jesus Christ] is not condemned; but he who does not believe is condemned already, because he has not believed in the name of the only begotten Son of God." This verse plainly establishes the fact that the destiny (eternal abode) of unbelievers is not decided at the great white throne (which is discussed below), but is dependent upon whether he accepts or rejects Christ as Savior during his lifetime upon the earth. The judgment of the great white throne concerns an assessment of the degree of guilt and determines the punishment due. This statement does not refer to the judgment of the nations for their treatment of Israel, Christ's "brethren," as described in Matthew 25:31-46, where the "sheep" are separated from the "goats."

There are two judgments that are of vital importance to those now living on the earth. They are the *judgment seat of Christ,* which is only for believers, those who receive Christ as Savior during their lifetime upon the earth, and the *judgment of the great white throne,* which is for those who reject the Lord Jesus Christ as Savior during their lifetime upon the earth. Following is a discussion of these two judgments.

The Judgment Seat of Christ

This occurs between the rapture and the marriage of the Lamb. It concerns believers only. The marriage supper follows the marriage and is distinct from the marriage, others being invited who are not involved in the marriage (Rev. 19:6-9). According to 2 Corinthians 5:10, all believers must stand before the judgment seat of Christ to give account—"that each one may receive the things done in the body, according to what he has done, whether good or bad." (Note, Romans 14:10-12 references the judgment seat of Christ as well, but a number of translations render it "the judgment seat of *God*"). See also Revelation 22:12, which applies to members of the church. This is not a judgment for punishment, but for recompense—to receive rewards for faithfulness and to suffer loss for things not done to the glory of God; rather, it is a measure of faithfulness, of stewardship. Everyone present shall give account of himself to God. This is the subject of 1 Corinthians 3:10-15. In 1 Corinthians 6:19-20, the reader is admonished to glorify God in his body. The judge who shall preside at this judgment and also at the great white throne is the Lord Jesus, for God has committed all judgment to Him (see John 5:22-27). In the light of John 17:24, we know that Christ desires our companionship throughout eternity, but He is just and everything that is unworthy in each believer must be dealt with—not for punishment, but for reward. "There is therefore now no condemnation to those who are in Christ Jesus" (Rom. 8:1). Two other verses are worthy of consideration here: 1 Corinthians 11:31 and 1 John 1:9.

The Judgment of The Great White Throne

No one who refuses to trust the Lord Jesus Christ as Savior during their life on earth (neglecting or failing to trust Him amounts to a refusal) will escape this awesome judgment. The Lord Jesus Himself will be the Judge—no longer will He offer salvation to those who would trust Him, as the time when He would forgive them (the day of grace) will be past. This judgment is fully described in Revelation 20:11-15 in all the dreadful horror and finality of its results. The decisions are irreversible. It need only be emphasized that the consignment to the lake of fire is forever, without any hope or possibility of deliverance in spite of the love and longsuffering of God as recorded in John 3:16 and 2 Peter 3:9. God has warned that, apart from faith in the Lord Jesus as Savior, man has no hope for eternity (John 3:36; Heb. 10:28-31). God shows the certainty of all this by listing who must have their place in the lake of fire in Revelation 21:8; these ones cannot enter heaven (Rev. 21:27).

Other Judgments

There are a number of other judgments recorded in the Bible. In some cases it is difficult to know the exact time of these, but they are listed below with references to where they are mentioned.

- The judgment of the living Gentile nations after the great tribulation and before the millennial reign of Christ (Rev. 19:11; Matt. 25:31-46; Acts 17:31).
- Judgment of Israel (possibly the great tribulation is part of this judgment, Rev. 6:17), "the time of Jacob's trouble" (Jer. 30:7). See Malachi 3–4; Matthew 19:28 and chs. 24–25; Luke 22:30; and Revelation 1:7.
- Beast and false prophet cast into lake of fire (Rev. 19:20).
- The devil bound and cast into the bottomless pit (Rev. 20:1-3).
- The devil and the demons (the devil's angelic following) cast into the lake of fire—possibly at the same time the devil is consigned there (Rev. 12:9; 20:10; Matt. 25:41).

- Judgment of the angels that sinned with mankind before the flood; they "did not keep their proper domain" (Gen. 6:1-6; 1 Cor. 6:3; 2 Peter 2:4; Jude 6). Their judgment may be at the same time the devil is cast into the lake of fire.

What is Armageddon? Will Christians be there?

The name *Armageddon* occurs just once in the Bible, in Revelation 16:16. Many Bible students think it is the awful holocaust recorded in Ezekiel 38–39, after which it requires seven years to burn the instruments of war and seven months to bury the dead. It is the coming together of the kings of the earth and the whole world against God—"the battle of that great day of God Almighty" (Rev. 16:14), the final rebellion at the end of the great tribulation. The word *Armageddon* is interpreted as meaning the mountain of Megiddo. It appears that the battle will be fought in the plains of Jezreel, or Esdraelon.

The battle is described in Revelation 19:11-21. The Lord comes forth from heaven, the Rider of the white horse, accompanied by the "armies which were in heaven" (Rev. 19:11-16)—armies composed of the bride of the Lamb, the guests that were at the marriage supper of the Lamb (Old Testament saints), and possibly the angels (Matt. 25:31): all clothed in fine linen, white and clean.

The victory belongs to He who rides the white horse, for He has the only weapon (v. 15), a fearsome weapon—it is enough! All the birds that fly in the midst of heaven are invited to a feast of the flesh of kings and captains and of mighty men, horses and them that sit on them, and the flesh of all men, both free and bond, both small and great, even before the battle begins. It is soon over—the beast and the false prophet whom the devil energized to assemble this vast army are cast alive into the lake of fire. The King of kings and Lord of lords will be victorious. An angel lays hold of the devil, binds him with a great chain and casts him into the bottomless pit for a thousand years, and the one-thousand-year reign of Christ begins after His dealing in judgment with the living nations and Israel.

Will Christians be there? Yes, as a part of the church, the bride, Christians will be at the battle of Armageddon and with the Lord throughout His millennial reign—ever safe. The redeemed shall be forever with the Lord.

What is the millennium?

The millennium is the one-thousand-year reign of Christ. The Lord Jesus will reign in peace and righteousness on the throne of David (Luke 1:32) after He has subdued all His enemies (Rev. 19:11 to Rev. 20:6). It follows the battle of Armageddon at the end of the tribulation. The beast and the false prophet will have been cast into the lake of fire; all the army of the wicked who rebelled against God will have been slain by the Lord, the King of kings and Lord of lords, the Rider on the white horse; the devil will have been bound with a great chain and cast into the bottomless pit for one thousand years of Christ's reign (Rev. 20:1-3). There will be total peace—the wolf and the lamb shall lie down together, the lion shall eat straw like the ox, they shall not hurt nor destroy—all will be peace (Isaiah 11; 65:9-25).

Unredeemed man never ceases to have a sinful heart, but during the millennium the presence of the Lord will restrain sin, and Satan will be bound, unable to stir men up. Human life will last much longer—so much so that if one dies at a hundred years of age, he will be considered a mere child (Isa. 65:20).

The description of this one-thousand year reign is given in Revelation 20:4-6. But even after this reign of peace there will still be multitudes whose hearts are evil. When the devil is released from the bottomless pit, he will deceive the nations and gather an army together to fight against the saints and against God—an army described as great in number as the sand of the sea. But fire will come down from God out of heaven and devour them. The devil that deceived them will be cast forever into the lake of fire and brimstone to join the beast and the false prophet and shall be tormented day and night forever and ever (Rev. 20:7-10).

After the devil is cast into the lake of fire, the wicked dead will be raised and judged according to their works and cast into the lake of fire as their final eternal destination (Rev. 20:7-15; 21:8) as described under the paragraph above, the judgment of the great white throne. The "eternal state" will follow.

What is "the eternal state"?

The eternal state is a term used to describe an unending enjoyment of peace and righteousness by the redeemed with the Lord. The church, the bride of the Lamb, will be with Him in heaven forever, serving Him and reigning (1 Thess. 4:16-17; Rev. 22:1-5). It also seems, based on Revelation 19, that the Old Testament saints, although not a part of the church, will have their place in heaven as well. Revelation 21:1 is most interesting: "And I saw a new heaven and a new earth, for the first heaven and the first earth had passed away. Also, there was no more sea." Obviously the heaven referred to is not God's home but the space above us, as in Genesis 1:8. The fact that there will be no more sea means much more area for habitation, as 70 percent of the present earth is sea.

There will be a vast multitude (both Jews and Gentiles) saved during the great tribulation period who will not be part of the church. There are many things in the closing chapters of Revelation that seem to indicate that they will dwell on the new earth. God will yet fulfill His promises to Abraham concerning His earthly people, Israel. This is a tremendous study in itself and cannot be undertaken here. Consider one Scripture: Romans 11:26, "And so all Israel shall be saved: as it is written, There shall come out of Zion the Deliverer, and shall turn away ungodliness from Jacob"—see Isaiah 59:20 and chapter 60.

The Lord (spoken of as "Jesus" in Luke 1:31-33 and "the Lamb" in Rev. 22:3) will reign over all for ever—"of His kingdom there shall be no end" (Luke 1:33). But there is no competition in the Godhead: "And when all things shall be subdued unto Him, then shall the Son also Himself be subject unto Him that put all things under Him, that God may be all in all" (1 Cor. 15:28).

In the eternal state,

- We shall be satisfied (Ps. 17:15)
- We shall have fullness of joy and pleasures for evermore (Ps. 16:11)
- We shall be with Christ and like Him (1 Thess. 4:16-17; John 14:1-3; 17:24; 1 John 3:2)
- We shall serve the Lord (Rev. 22:3)
- We shall see Him and know we are His (1 John 3:2; Rev. 22:4)
- We shall reign forever (Rev. 22:5)
- There will be no tears, sorrow, crying, pain, death (Rev. 21:3-4), or evil (Rev. 21:8)
- All will praise the Lamb (Jesus) without one dissenting voice (Phil. 2:9-11; Rev. 5:11-14)

- God shall be all in all (1 Cor. 15:24-28)
- It will be more than anyone can imagine (1 Cor. 2:9-11)
- There will be no night, and no sin (Rev. 21:25-27).

Amen! Even so, come, Lord Jesus (Rev. 22:20).

Bibliography

BOOKS SUGGESTED FOR further study on the subjects addressed in this booklet:

We Believe in Biblical Inerrancy—C. C. Ryrie, Dallas Theological Seminary

Rightly Dividing the Word of Truth—C. I. Scofield, ECS Ministries

God's Good News—A. P. Gibbs, ECS Ministries

God's Answers to Man's Questions—William MacDonald, ECS Ministries

Securely Saved and Sure of It—Ken Fleming, ECS Ministries

The Person and Work of the Holy Spirit—S. Ridout, Loizeaux Brothers

Eternal Security of the Believer—H. A. Ironside

Christ Loved the Church—William MacDonald, ECS Ministries

I Will Build My Church—James Gunn, ECS Ministries

The Christian Assembly—J. R. Littleproud, Gospel Folio Press

Bishops, Priests, and Deacons—W. Hoste, Pickering & Inglis

Christian Baptism—A. P. Gibbs, ECS Ministries

The Lord's Supper—A. P. Gibbs, ECS Ministries

Worship, the Christian's Highest Occupation—A. P. Gibbs, ECS Ministries

The Holy Trinity—H. A. Ironside, Loizeaux Brothers

Satan, the Prince of Darkness—F. A. Tatford, Kregel

Things to Come—J. Dwight Pentecost, Zondervan

ECS Booklets

Angels
Armageddon Soon?
Assurance of Salvation
Baptism: The Church's Troubled Water
Basic Doctrines of the Christian Faith
Blessed Trinity
The Challenge of Change in Assembly Missions
Child Evangelism
Christian Devotedness
The Christian Woman in God's Family and Church
Church Discipline
Cremation: Is It Christian?
Divorce and the Bible
Fundamental, Important, and Non-Essential Issues
God's Answers to Man's Questions
God's Good News
The Grace of God in Salvation
Grasping for Shadows
An Introduction to a Study of Church Truth
Is Jesus Christ Lord?
The Lord's Supper: The Church's Love Feast
Men Who Met Jesus
Our Reason To Be
The Principle of Work
Principles & Rewards of Giving
Seek Ye First
The Seven C's of Decision Making
That's a Good Question!
There's a Way Back to God
Think of Your Future
To What Should We Be Loyal?
True Brokenness
What's Life All About?
Who Is the Greatest Man Alive?
Your Mind Matters

ECS eBooklets

